A Year in the Garden

by Joanna Lake

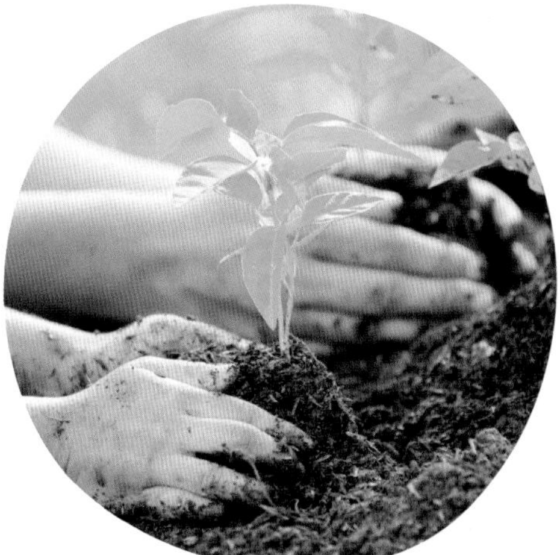

OXFORD
UNIVERSITY PRESS
AUSTRALIA & NEW ZEALAND

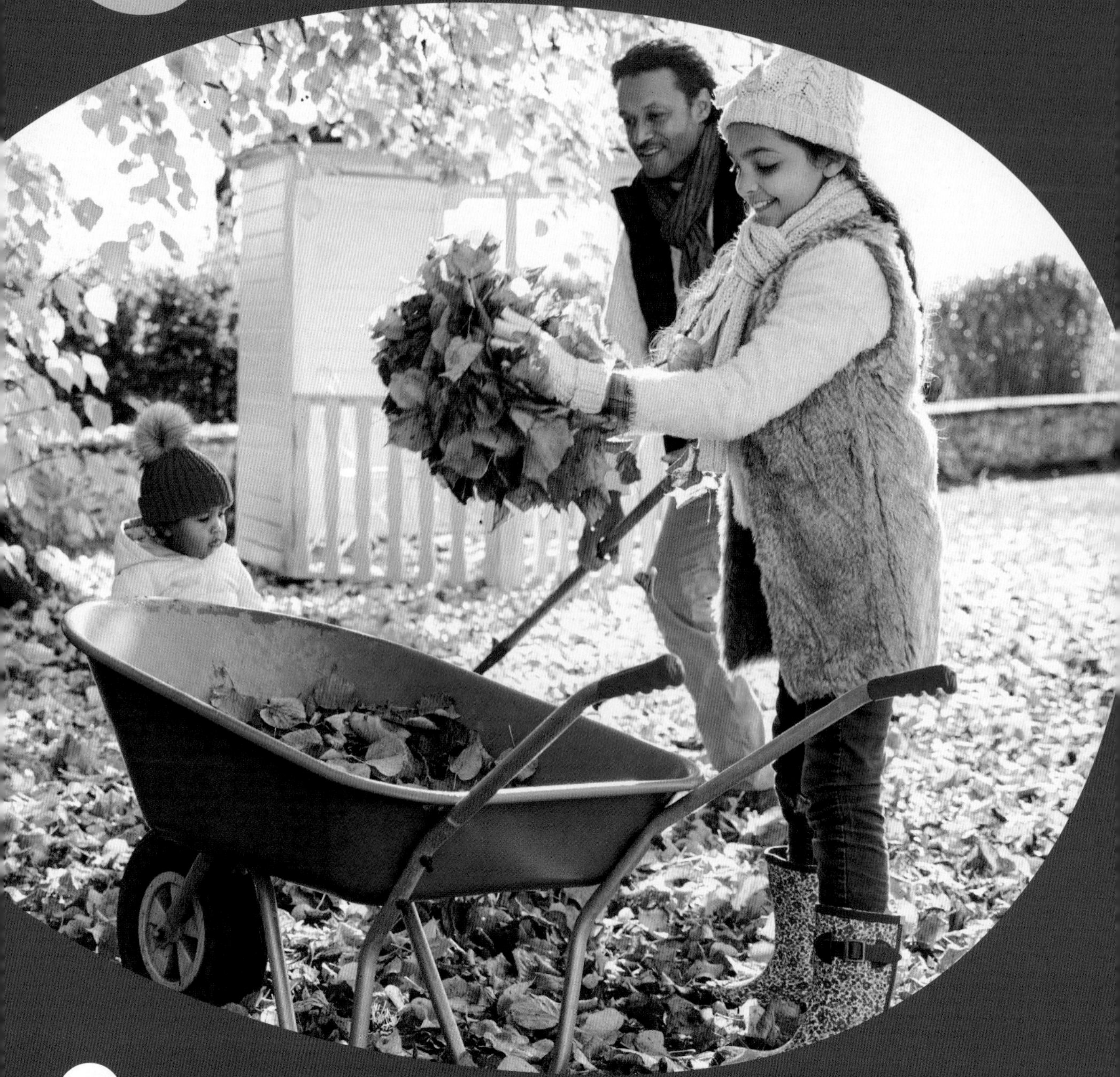

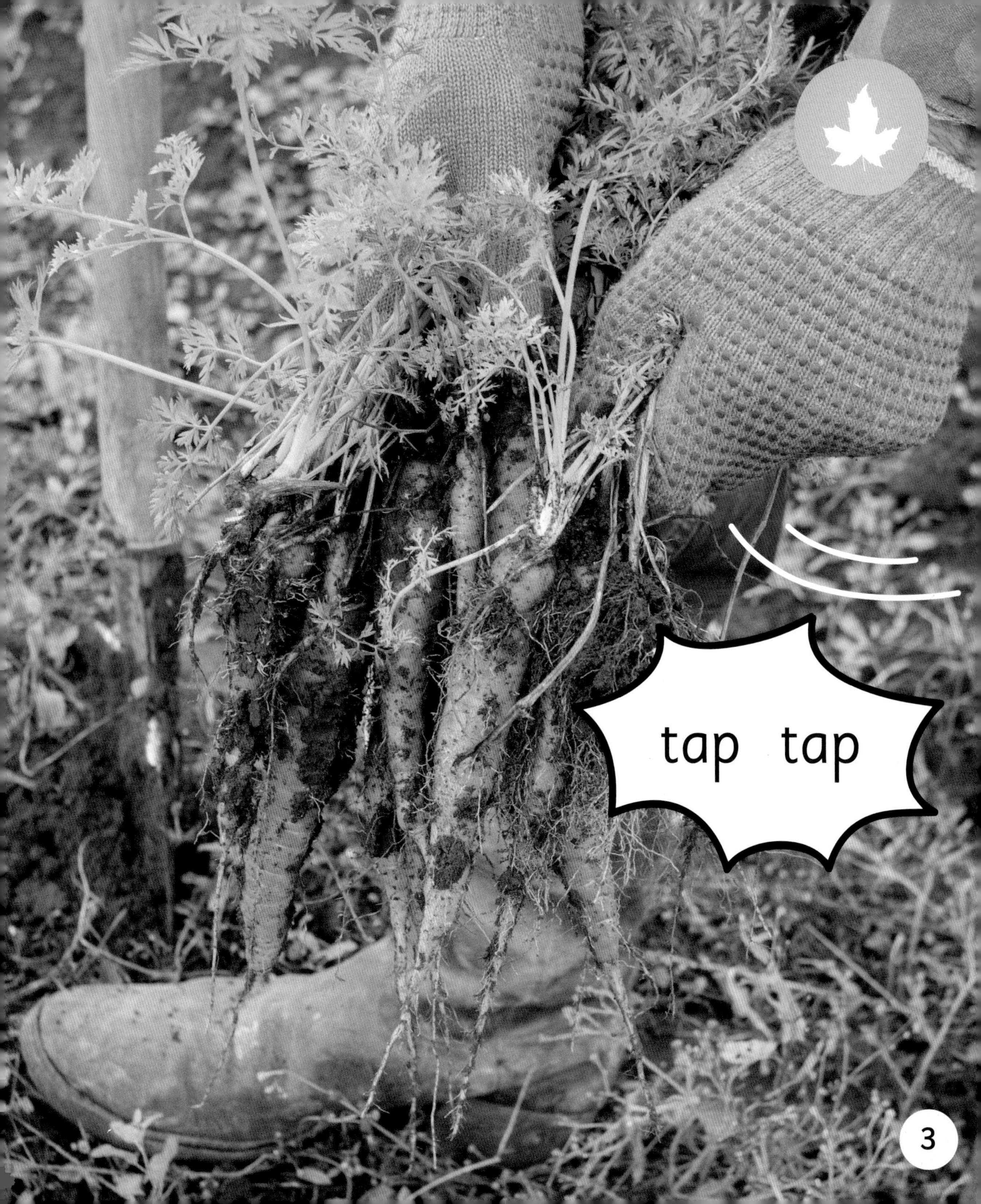
tap tap

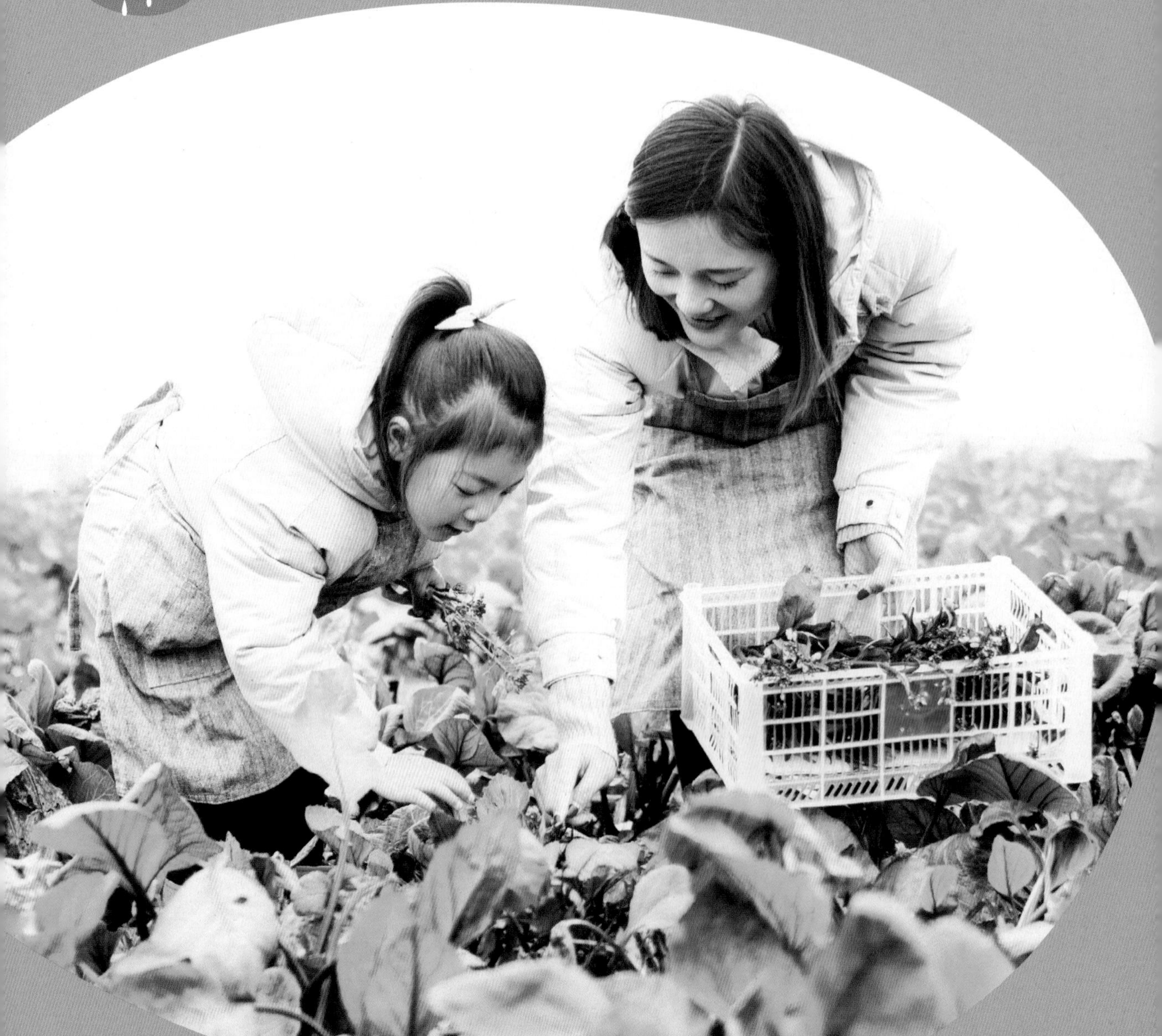

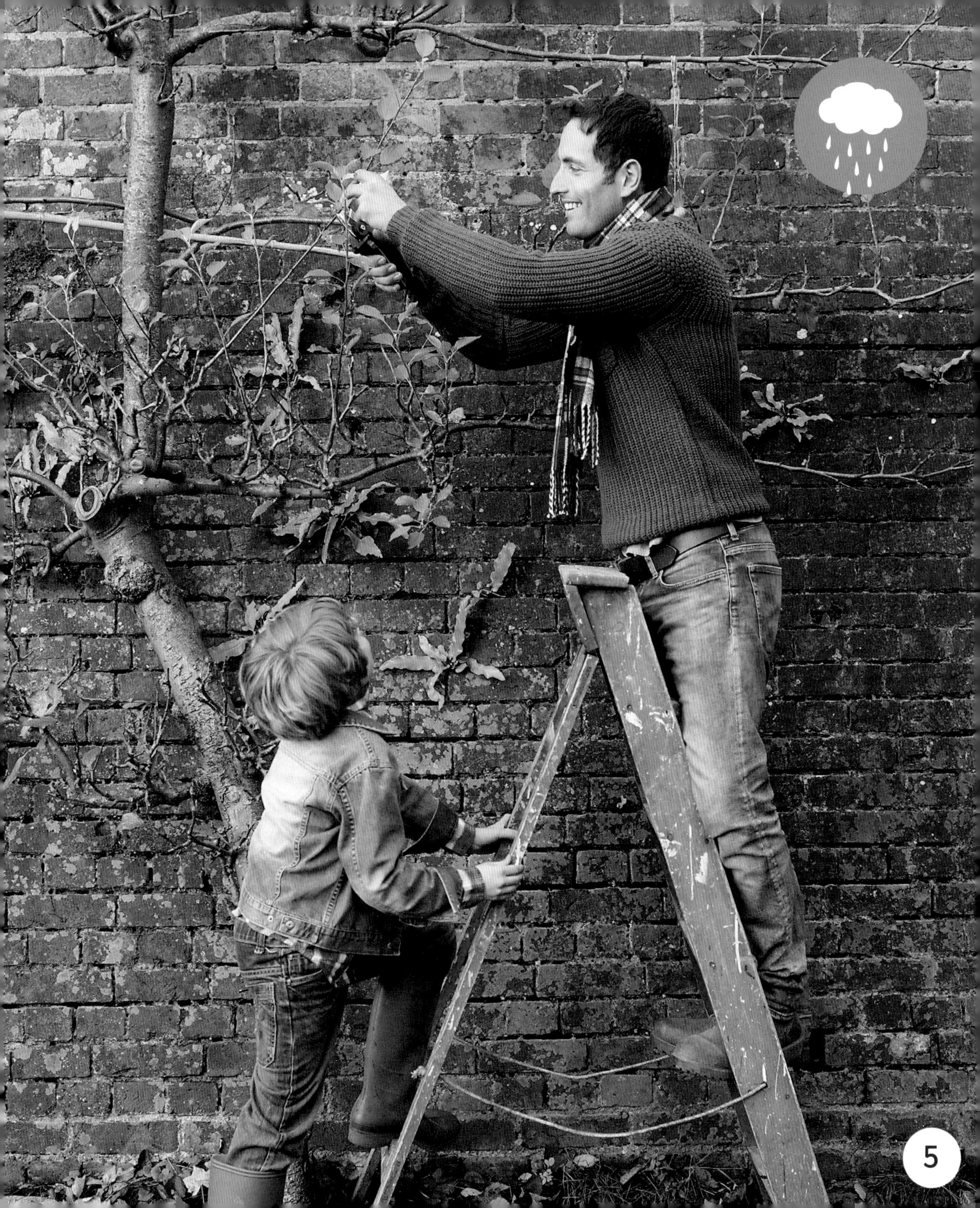

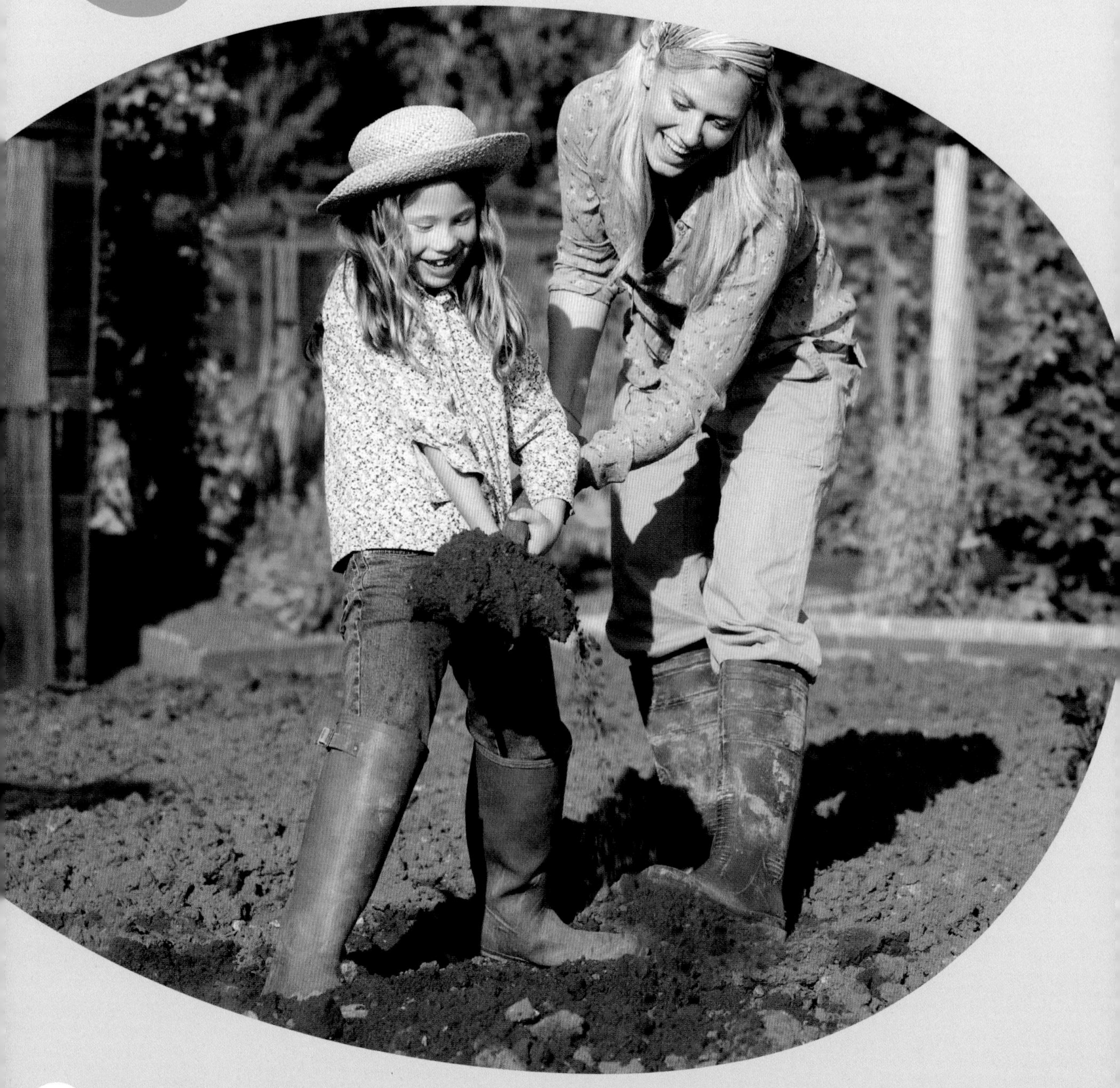

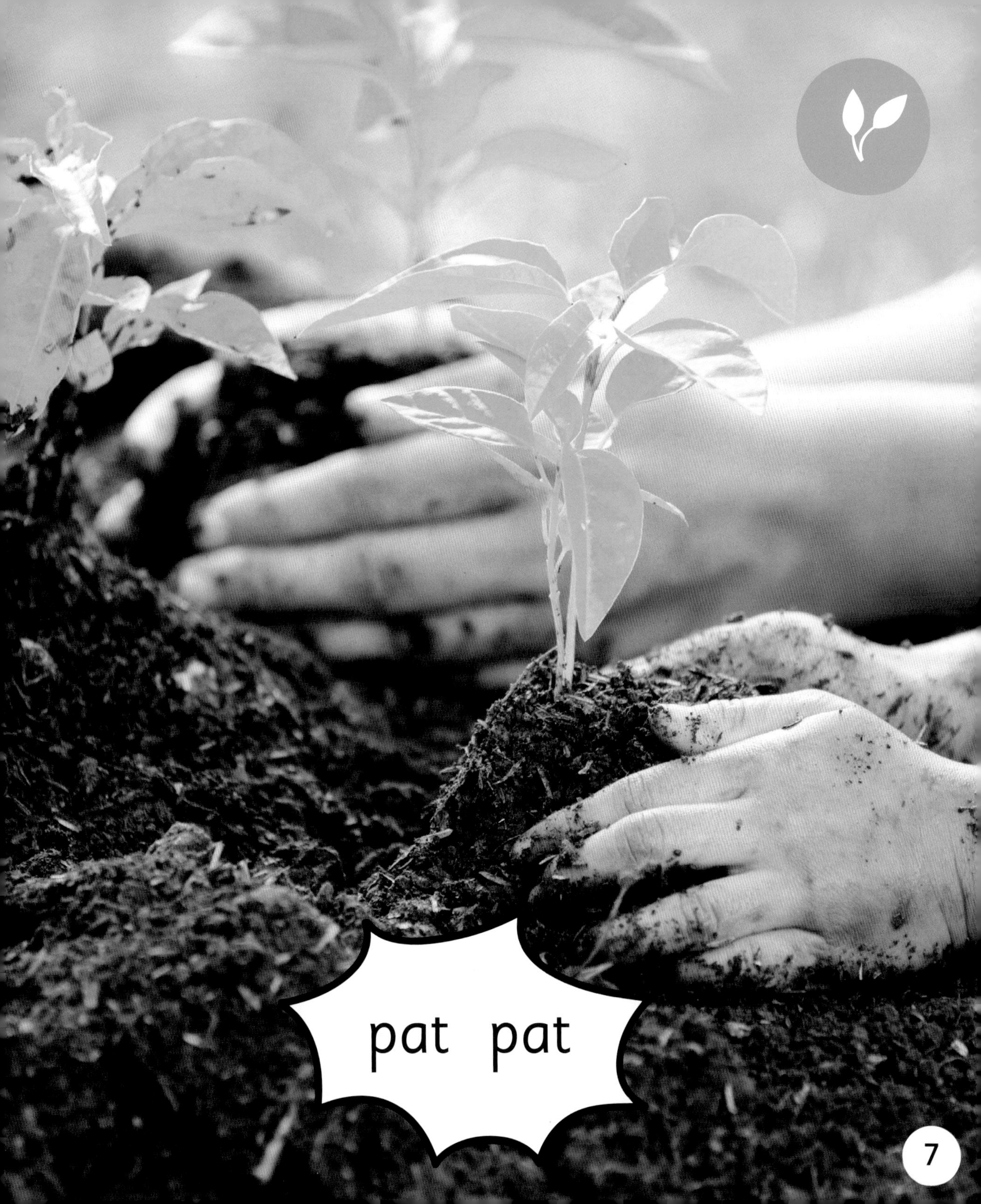

pat pat

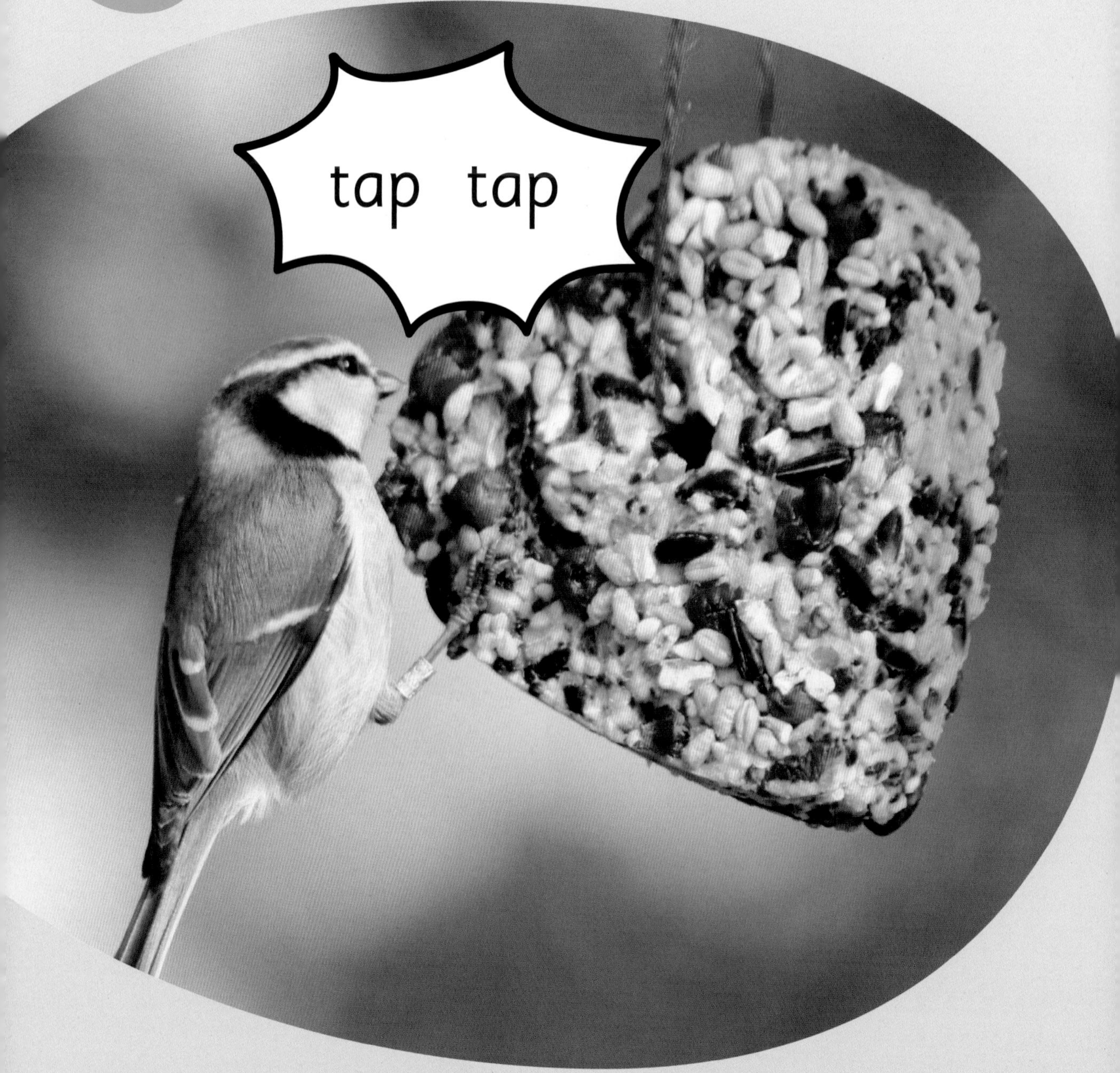
tap tap

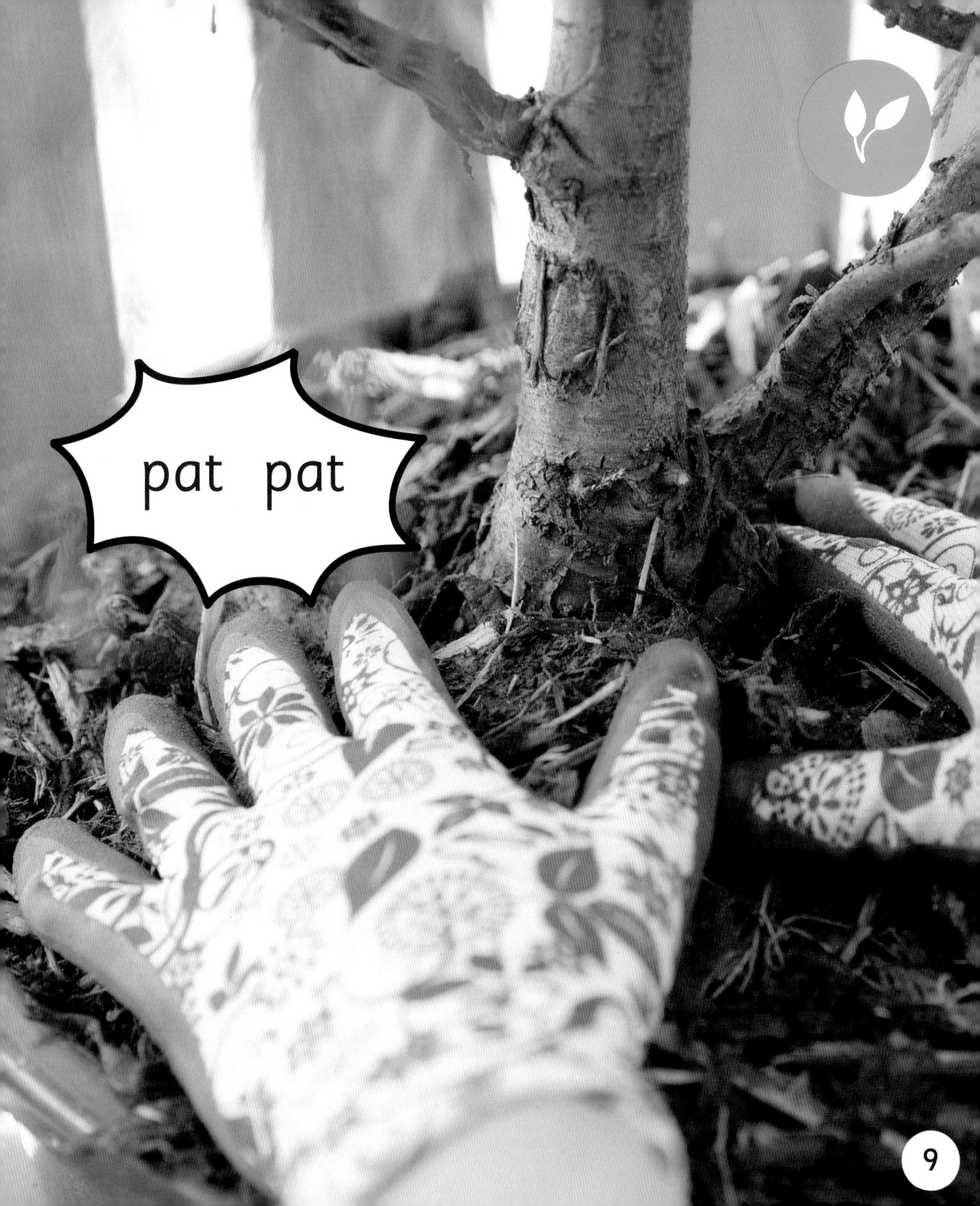
pat pat

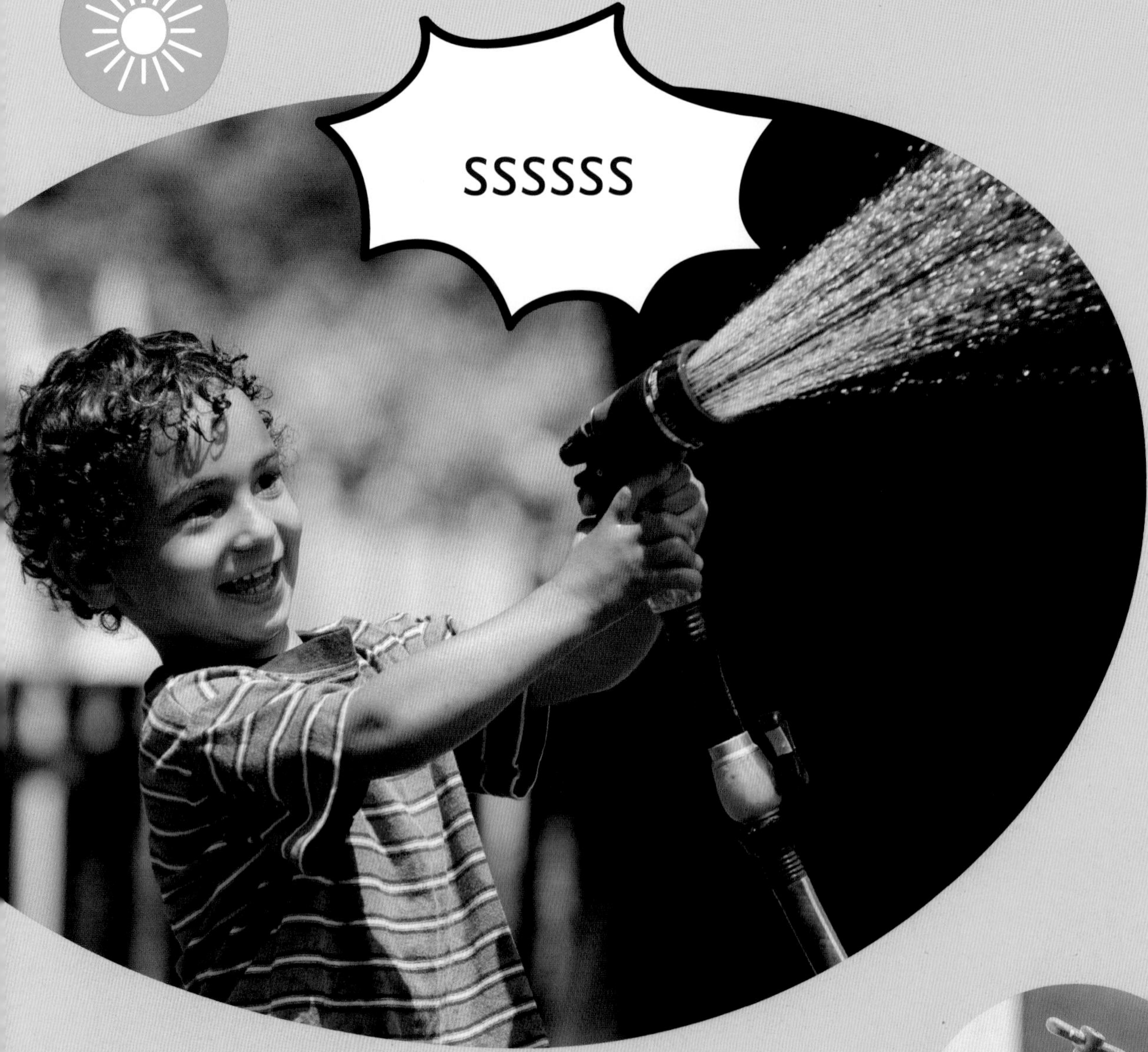
ssssss

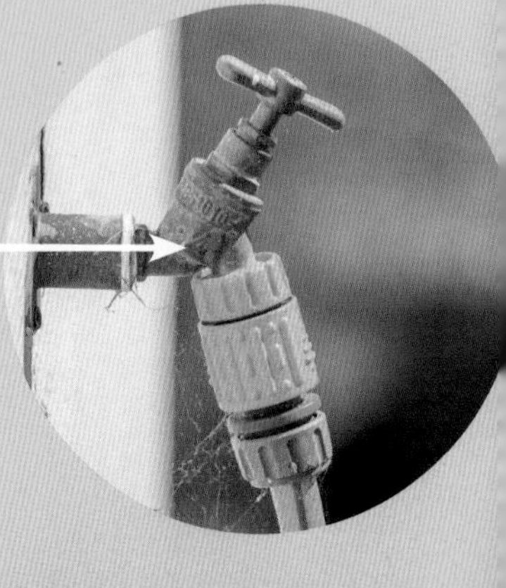
tap

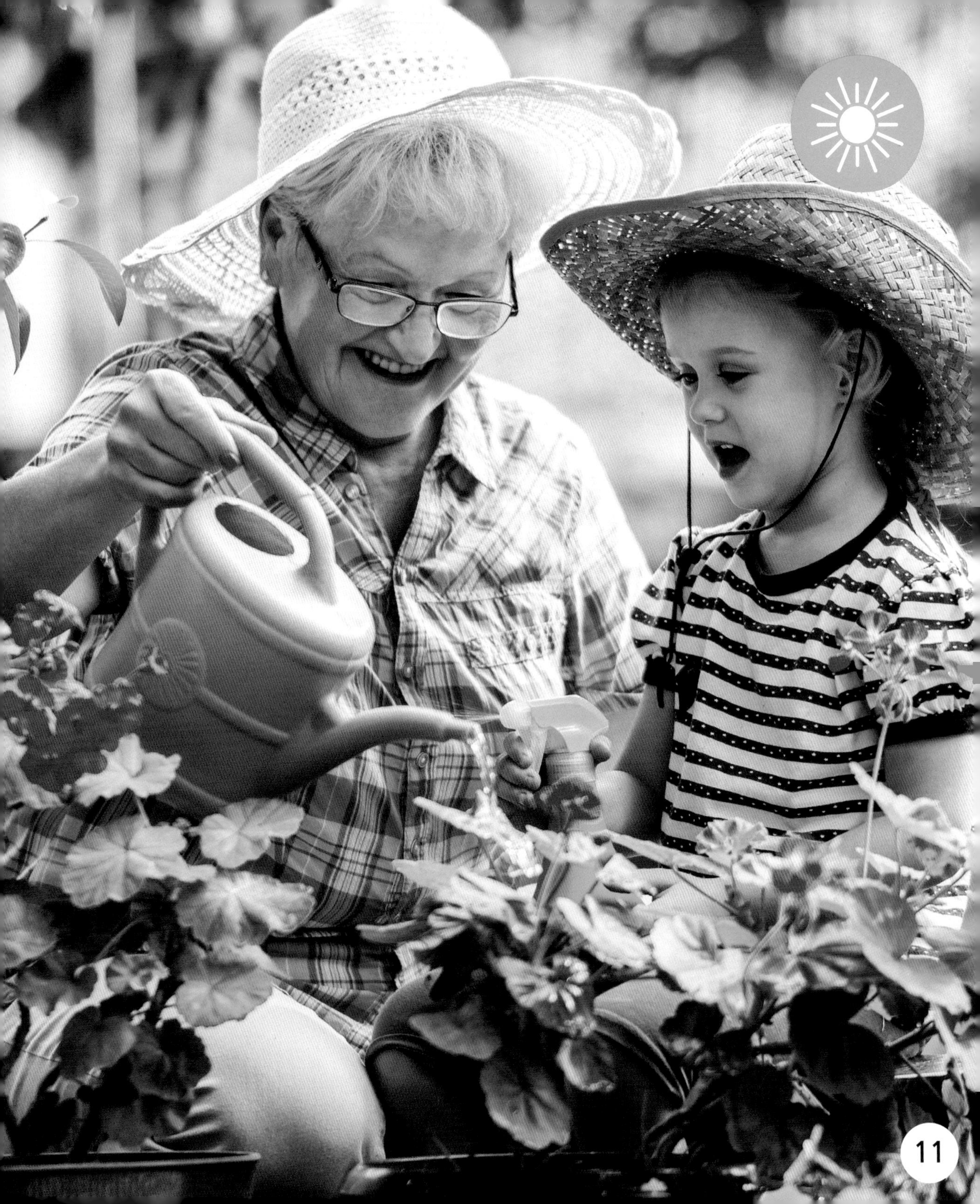

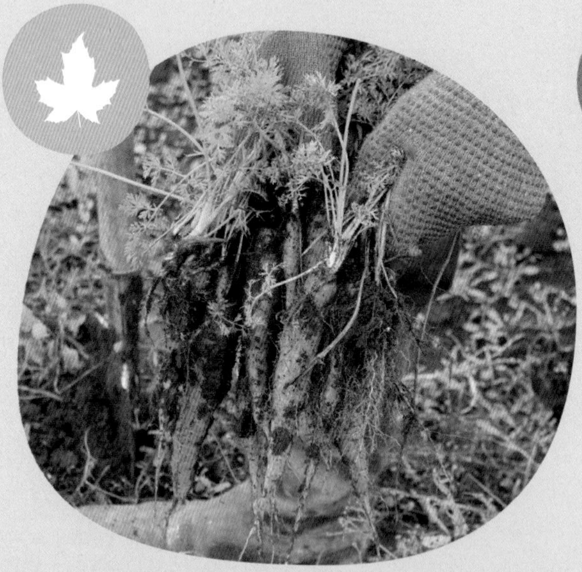
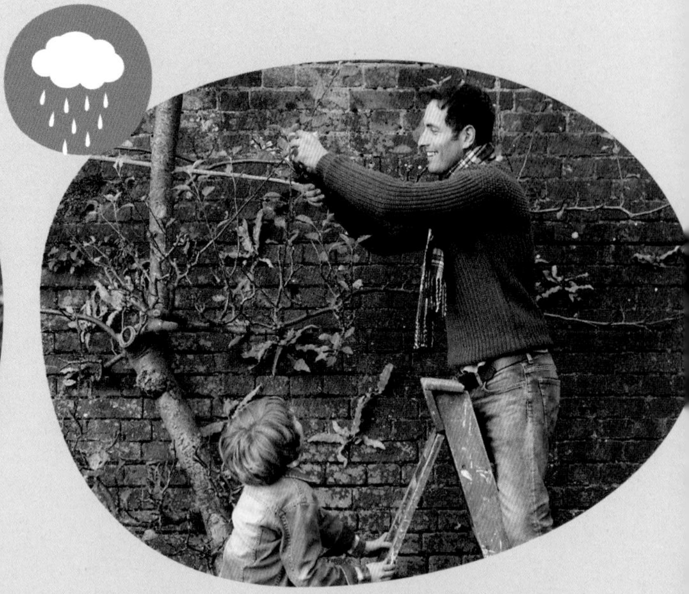
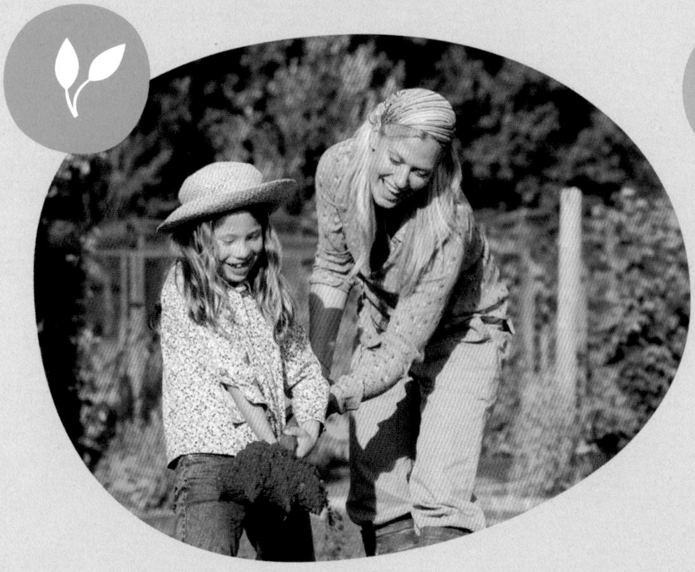
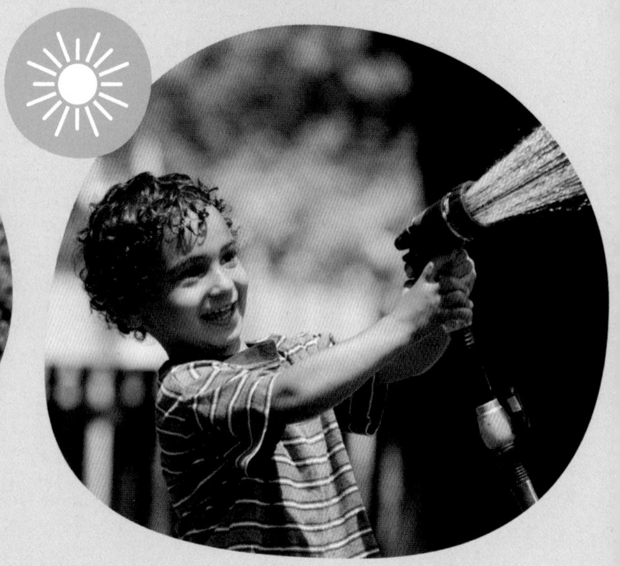